# Children's Reiki Handbook

# CHILDREN'S REIKI HANDBOOK

A Guide to Energy Healing for Kids

Pamela A. Yarborough
and Robert T. Yarborough

Second Edition
Revised and Expanded

Andborough Publishing • Colorado

Andborough Publishing
4935 Sprangler Drive
Colorado Springs, Colorado 80922
USA



First Edition November 2005
Second Edition Revised February 2007



*Publishers Cataloging-in-Publication Data*

Yarborough, Pamela A. 1957-
Children's Reiki Handbook: A Guide to Energy Healing for Kids / Pamela A. and Robert T. Yarborough: Photography by Robert T. Yarborough–2nd ed.
p.cm
Includes index
ISBN # 978-0-9774181-5-2
1. Reiki (Healing system). 2. Reiki-Children. 3. Healing-Energy.
I. Yarborough, Robert T., joint author. II. Title.

Library of Congress Control Number: 2007901597

Printed in the United States of America

*Dedicated*
*with love*
*to all our children*

# CONTENTS

# CONTENTS (CONTINUED)

# NOTE TO READERS

(Disclaimer and other nonsense)

Healing and medicine are two very different disciplines. The information in this book is not medicine, it is healing and does not constitute medical advice.

The contents of this book, such as text, graphics, and other material are for informational purposes only and are not intended as a substitute for professional medical/dental advice, diagnosis, or treatment.

Always seek the advice of your physician, dental professional or other legally licensed and qualified health care provider with any questions you may have regarding a medical/dental condition. Never disregard professional medical/dental advice or delay in seeking it because of content found in this book.

If you have a medical/dental emergency, call your physician/dentist or 911 immediately. Reliance on any information provided the authors and/or the publishers, is solely at your own risk.

I feel truly sad that our country has progressed to the point that I must make a disclaimer to avoid possible harassment and prosecution from our government of the people, in the form of the Federal Trade Commission and the Federal Drug Administration, for expressing my constitutional right of free speech. Because, in this book I have expressed my genuine belief that all people have the power to heal themselves and others.

So my best advice to you is to not believe anything that you read here; but can I say "not believe" without another disclaimer?

# Preface

Almost everything in my life revolves around my family and most importantly, my children. So it was no different when I began my Reiki journey; my children were involved as well. Once I was attuned as a Reiki Master and Teacher I felt a calling to teach Reiki to children.

Although I received much advice and numerous warnings that I should not teach Reiki to children, for fear that it would somehow "damage" them or be too "overwhelming" for them, I knew this was the farthest thing from the truth. In fact I felt then, and have since witnessed, that exposing children to Reiki creates a greater awareness of themselves and guides them to a life of compassion.

The first version of this book was a simple hand-out I created for my students to provide them with something to use during their initial class and attunement, and to take home to use as a reference. The second version, that was to become the first published edition was created with much help from my husband Robert.

Of course as we both continued our journey with Reiki we discovered that we, as many others in America, were taught an incorrect history of Reiki. This, and the desire to increase the scope of the book, lead to this revised and expanded 2nd edition of the book.

But as with the first edition, this is not a book of new knowledge. It is rather, an arrangement of existing knowledge from many sources into a concise presentation of what children should know about basic energy healing to help prepare them for Level One, Level Two and Master Reiki Attunements.

This book includes a brief study of the fundamentals of the energy of our bodies, auras, chakras, basic energy healing principles, healing hand positions, and distant healing techniques that will allow the child to practice energy healing on family, friends, and pets.

Happy healing,

*Pamela Yarborough*

# Children's Reiki Handbook

# CHAPTER 1
# WHAT IS REIKI?

*"Our Reiki Ryoho is something absolutely original and cannot be compared with any other (spiritual) path in the world."*

- Mikao Usui
(Founder of Usui Reiki Ryoho)

The word reiki is used to describe many types of healing and spiritual work. One type of reiki, or system of healing, is the Usui (Ewe shoe e) method. This is the system of healing you will learn about in this book. It is called the Usui System of Natural Healing or in Japanese, Usui Reiki Ryoho.

The word "reiki" combines the two Japanese words, rei (ray) which means "spirit" or "soul," and ki (key) means "energy," or "life force". So in English, reiki (ray key) means "Universal Life Force."

Learning Reiki is really rather simple and it doesn't matter how smart you are, or how fast you learn, or what language you speak, or what religion you believe. The ability to use Reiki is available to everyone! It has been taught to thousands of people of all ages and backgrounds.

In Usui Reiki, practitioners channel and focus the

Universal Life Force from its source to themselves or to others who need its healing energy. The source of Reiki energy is the creation energy of the universe; the energy that creates all living things. Some people call this creator or god energy.

You can learn about Reiki from reading a book and you can practice the various hand positions until you know them, but the ability to use Reiki is not learned the same way you learn other new things such as jumping rope or riding a bike. Reiki, and the ability to use Reiki energy to help others, is transferred to you by a Reiki Master during a ceremony called an attunement. You'll learn about attunements later.

## Who Started Usui Reiki?

Mikao Usui is the founder of the Usui System of Reiki. He was born 15 August 1865 in the Yamagata district of Gifu prefecture, Japan. Usui was born into a samurai family and were hatamoto; one of the highest ranks within the samurai class.

Mikao Usui

As a samurai, Usui began studying the martial art of aikijutsu at an early age and attained the highest rank in his mid-twenties. He was also friendly with some of the great martial artist of his time including Gichin Funakoshi (founder of modern karate), Jigoro Kano (founder of Judo) and Moreihei Ueshiba (founder of Aikido).

He was a life long learner and worked hard at his studies. Some of the subjects he learned included history, medicine, psychology, and religion. After he grew up he visited Europe, America and studied in China.

Meditation was always part of Usui's life and it was during meditation that he gained the power to heal. It was during a 21-day program of meditation on Mount Kurama, that he attained enlightenment and the secrets to his Reiki Ryoho.

From this moment on he was able to heal and used his powers to heal himself and his family. But Usui thought that is was better use his healing powers on the general public than to just use on himself and his family. And in April of 1922 he began to teach Reiki Ryoho and give treatments to the sick.

On 11 April 1922 Usui opened a clinic in Harajuku, Aoyama, Tokyo. He gave treatment to patients and held workshops to teach others about Reiki. By 1925 he had so many patients he had to build a new clinic in Nakano just outside of Tokyo.

Several years after developing Reiki, Usui added the Reiki Precepts (rules to guide your behavior), to the practice of Reiki. These were developed to add spiritual balance to Usui Reiki.

Their purpose is to help people realize that improving yourself is a necessary part of the Reiki healing. To have lasting results, the person you are healing must accept responsibility for their own healing through self-improvement.

Just for today,

do not anger,

do not worry

be grateful

be honest in your work

be kind to others.

Do gassho every morning and evening

Keep the precepts in mind throughout the day.

Improve your body and mind

- Usui Mikao

## Who Brought Reiki to the West?

There are two people who we must give credit for bringing Reiki to the Western World. Dr. Chujiro Hayashi and Hawayo Takata.

Chujiro Hayashi

Dr Chujiro Hayashi

Chujiro Hayashi was a medical doctor and a Reiki Master student of Usui. Because of his medical background he was asked by Usui to create the Reiki Ryoho Hikkei (Spiritual Energy Healing Method Manual) and is credited for adding the hand positions for treating different illnesses to the manual.

After Usui's death, Dr. Hayashi actively promoted Reiki throughout Japan. He opened his own Reiki clinic in Tokyo and he became very well know among the most affluent people.

Dr. Hayashi's more structured version of Usui's system of healing is the Reiki system that was first taught in the West.

Hawayo Takata

During a visit to Japan, Hawayo Takata, a Hawaiian born Japanese, needed medical care and went to a hospital in Tokyo. While being prepared for surgery, her inner voice told her that she didn't need the operation. When she asked about an alternative, she was referred her to Dr. Hayashi's Reiki Clinic.

After receiving daily Reiki treatments at the Reiki Clinic she was initiated to Shoden, or Level One Reiki, so that she could perform self-treatments. After six months she was cured.

She spent a year as a student and intern in the clinic before returning to her home in Hawaii. Several weeks later Dr. Hayashi and his daughter traveled to Hawaii to help Takata build her Reiki practice. Dr. Hayashi stayed for six months and just before his return to Japan he announced that Takata was a Master of the Usui System of Natural Healing. She was his thirteenth Master student.

Takata traveled around the Hawaiian Islands for the next 30 years healing and teaching. She taught 22 of her students to Master level.

# Chapter 2
# Your Energy Body

*"Keeping your body healthy is an expression of gratitude to the whole cosmos - the trees, the clouds, everything."*

- Thich Nhat Hanh
(Zen Master, scholar, poet, peace activist, and author of over 60 books)

Since ancient times many cultures believed that there is an unseen energy or life force that flows throughout all living creatures. In the movie Star Wars, Obi Wan Kenobi explains the "Force" as "... an energy field created by all living things. It surrounds us and penetrates us. It binds the galaxy together." But this is not a myth from ancient folklore or something invented for the movies, modern scientists have verified the existents of this energy force.

This energy force is created from the vibrations given off by all things in the universe. These vibrations come from the movement of electrons and protons of every atom of every molecule found in everything. The more animated an object is, the greater the vibrations or higher the energy level. Plants have an overall higher energy level than rocks, but animals have higher energy than plants.

This energy or universal life force is known by many different names such as chi in China, ki in Japan, and prana in India, and many others.

## Your Aura

The energy created by the vibrations of your body is your energy body and is sometimes called your auric field or your Aura. Your Aura reflects a lot of information about you. The overall size, shape, number of colors and their shade and position can tell a lot about you. Your Aura can show how healthy you are physically, mentally, emotionally, and spiritually.

The size, shape, and colors of your Aura are unique to you and are changing and moving constantly. The colors that you radiate are affected by your well being, your physical surroundings, and by the people you come in contact with and the energy or vibrations they radiate. You will have main colors in your aura that reflect your primary personality traits. The chart on page 11 shows the colors associated with personality types and traits.

The size of your aura is also affected by your personality and emotions. If you are a shy or quite person, or you don't like to draw attention to yourself, or if you are in a depressed mood, your aura may extend only a few inch from your body. But if you are an out-going person and like to be the center of attention, or in a super energetic mood, your aura could extend out many feet away from your body.

## Seeing Your Aura

How do you know what your aura looks like if you can't see it? There are special equipment and cameras, such as a Kirlian camera, that are capable of recording your aura. There are even some people who can see auras. But even if you can't find someone with the equipment or who can see your aura, you can still feel the energy or vibrations of your aura.

You may not realize it but you sense vibrations all the time. When you choose your friends you sense that their vibrations are similar to your own. When we meet someone for the first time we can tell what they are like by the vibrations they are sending out. When you find a particular rock or sea shell that "feels" right to you, it probably has a vibration energy that is in harmony with your energy at that particular moment.

What are your favorite colors? Your favorite colors are probably the same colors as your main aura colors.

| Personality Color Chart | |
|---|---|
| Aura Color | Personality Characteristics |
| Deep-Red | Physical, hardworking, power, realistic, vital, grounded, strength, stamina |
| Red | Excitement, physical, energetic, competitive, winner, will-power, sexual, entrepreneur |
| Orange | Productive, physical and creative expression, adventurer, business, enjoyment |
| Yellow – Brown | Analytical, intellectual, detail oriented, logical, structured, scientific |
| Yellow | Playful, sunny, easy going, creative, intellectual, entertaining, curious, active |
| Green | Social, natural, content, harmony, teacher, communicative, quick minded |
| Deep-Green | Quick minded, goal-oriented, social, material, communicative, organizer |
| Blue | Caring, sensitive, loving, helpful, loyal, peaceful, desire to be of service, nurturing |
| Indigo | Clarity, calm, deep inner feelings, loving, loyal, introverted, inner values, artistic |
| Violet | Intuitive, artistic, sensual, theorist, futuristic, visionary, charismatic, innovative |
| Lavender | Imaginative, mystical, fantasy, soft, fragile, sensitive, often spacey, enteric |
| White | Transcendent, transformation, imaginative, quiet, higher dimensions, spiritual |

## Chakras

Our energy bodies have hundreds of energy centers that help us direct all the energy that is coming into and going out of our bodies and distribute the energy throughout our bodies for physical, emotional, mental, and spiritual functions. These energy centers are known as chakras. In Sanskrit the meaning of the word chakra is "spinning wheel of energy." Chakras are what helps link your physical body to your energy body.

Our bodies have seven major chakras that have the most energy activity with the energy body. These chakras correlate directly to parts of your physical body and are lined up from the crown of your head to the base of your spine. When these energy centers are all open and aligned it allows your universal life force to flow through them freely. Your hands and feet also contain chakras with lots of energy of activity.

Each chakra has its own natural or healthy vibration that corresponds to vibrations of certain colors, emotions, organs, nerve networks, sounds, and other elements. Here are the location and some of the characteristics of each chakra.

### Crown Chakra

The Crown Chakra is the seventh major chakra and is located at the top of the head. This is your spiritual center and is directed toward self-knowledge and pure awareness. It is your connection to a timeless and space less place of all-knowing. When balanced this chakra brings you knowledge, wisdom and spiritual connection. It works with all issues that affect you on a spiritual level and blend them with your earthly personality. The Crown Chakra's color is purple with white as the secondary color.

### Third Eye Chakra

The Third Eye Chakra is the sixth major chakra and is located on the brow of your head and is some times referred to as Brow Chakra. This is your psychic center and aids self-reflection. It can affect dreams, imagination, concentration, intuition, wisdom and clairvoyance. Clairvoyance is the ability to use your sixth sense or to "see" using senses beyond your five senses of touch, taste, hearing, smell, and sight.

The Third Eye Chakra represents the Light element and its color is indigo with purple as its secondary color. For your physical body it is associated with your ears, eyes, and nose as well as the glands in the upper facial region.

Location of the Seven Major Chakras

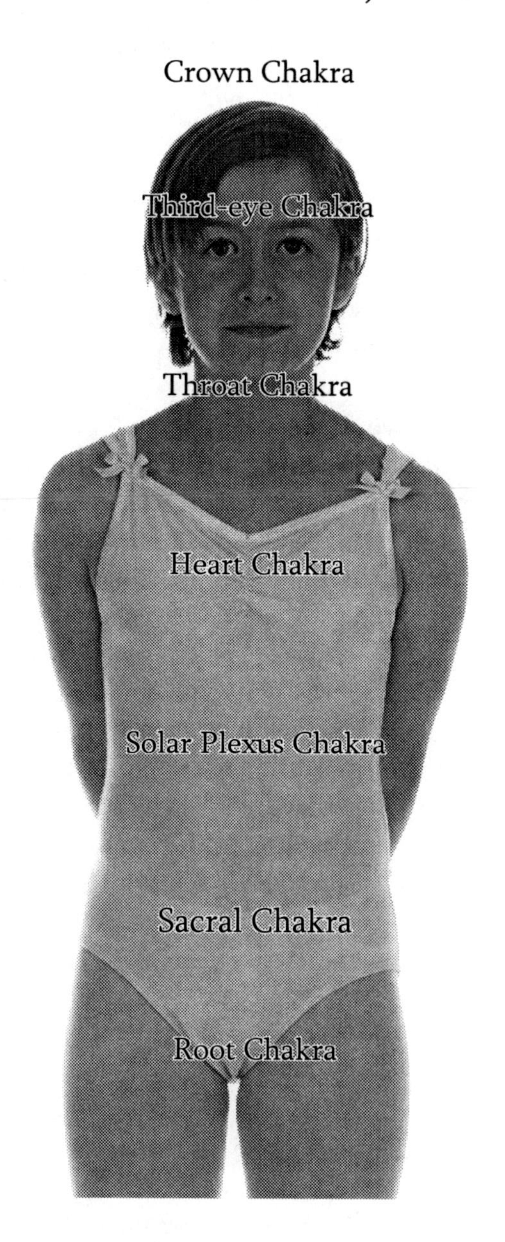

### Throat Chakra

The Throat Chakra is the fifth major chakra and is located in the throat area of your neck. This is your communication center and helps you deal with self-expression and your creative identity. It can also help improve clairaudience or the ability to hear spirit messages in thought form. You hear what they are saying in your mind. The Throat Chakra is represented by the element of sound and its color is blue. For your physical body it can affect the mouth, ears and upper respiratory system and is associated with the glands of the throat.

### Heart Chakra

The Heart Chakra is the fourth major chakra and is located in the center of your chest level with the heart. This is your emotional center and is the balance point of opposites of your psyche, such as mind and body, male and female, etc. It can help balance your emotions related to giving, receiving; losing and acquiring love; and help with your self-acceptance. A balanced heart chakra allows you to love deeply, feel compassion, and have a sense of center. It can also affect your clairsentience ability, or the ability to experience other realms with your sense of touch. The Heart Chakra represents the Air element and its color is green with pink as the secondary color. For your physical body it is associated with the heart, lungs, and circulation.

### Solar Plexus Chakra

The Solar Plexus Chakra is the third major chakra and is located in the solar plexus region. This is the center of your personal power and can help understand and increase your will power and autonomy. It also affects our energy, effectiveness, and spontaneity. The Solar Plexus Chakra represents the Fire element and its color is yellow. For your physical body it can aid digestion, and metabolism, and is associated with the nervous system, pancreas, gall bladder, liver, stomach and adrenal glands.

### Sacral Chakra

The Sacral Chakra is the second major chakra and is located in the lower abdomen at your spleen area. It is your instinct center and helps you develop your emotions and sexuality. It also helps with the connection with others through feelings, desires, and sensations, and with your ability to accept change. The Sacral Chakra represents the Water element and its color is orange. For your physical body it helps assimilate and process food and is associated with the spleen, genitals and bladder.

Root Chakra

The Root Chakra is the first of the seven major chakras and is located at the base of your spine. This is the center of self-preservation or survival instinct and your sense of grounding and the connection to the physical plane. This chakra brings us overall health, prosperity and sense of security. The Root Chakra represents the Earth element; and its color is red. For your physical body it is associated with the kidneys, adrenals, spinal column and colon.

## Feeling Our Energy Bodies

What are some other ways of feeling our energy? One way to feel energy is to rub your hands together really fast, like Mister Miyagi in the movie The Karate Kid. This opens up the palm chakras so you can feel your own energy and the energy of others.

After rubbing your hands together for 15 to 20 seconds, put your hands in front of you about two feet apart. Slowly move them together as close as you can without touching and then move them move them away from each other. After they are 5-6 inches apart, repeat the in and out movements; this will cause the energy to build-up between them. Pay attention to the difference in how your palms feel as you repeat this exercise; your hands are becoming more sensitive to small changes in energy.

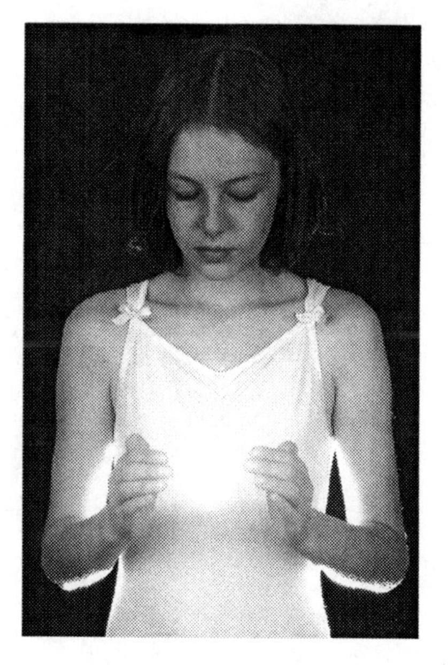

You can do this experiment with friends as well. Rub your hands together and then extend them out as if you were going to shake hands. When your hand gets close to your friend's hand, you should be able to feel their energy.

# Chapter 3
# Reiki Attunement Level One

*"Every patient carries her or his own doctor inside."*

- Albert Schweitzer (1875 - 1965)
(French philosopher & physician)

The Reiki Attunement is a special but simple ceremony that gives you the ability to use the Universal Life Force Energy to heal.

The attunement is the process to bring you into harmony with the universal life force. Your first level attunement will connect (attune) you to the source of reiki, open and clear your chakras so reiki can flow through them, and enable you to channel reiki to yourself and others.

After the attunement process you will always have Reiki. All you have to do is think about it and it will come to you. You will forever be able to use your healing energy to help all things that are living.

## Levels of Attunement and Reiki Symbols

In the classic, or original, Usui Reiki System there are three levels of attunement and four symbols used. The three levels of attunement are simply called the First Level Attunement, Second Level Attunement, and the Third Level or Master Attunement. During each of these attunements different Reiki symbols are placed in to your Crown, Heart and Palm Chakras and the symbols are activated, or turned on, for you to use.

The four Reiki symbols are the Energy Symbol, the Distant Healing Symbol, the Mental/Emotional Symbols, and the Master Symbol.

During your First Level Attunement the Energy Symbol is used to turn on your natural healing abilities. The Japanese name for this symbol is Cho Ku Rei.

The name Cho Ku Rei translates into "Put all the power in the universe here". Every time you draw this symbol you turn on your Reiki healing power.

Chokurei symbol can be used to increase the power of Reiki or to focus it on a specific part of the body. You can use the Energy Symbol at any time you are giving Reiki but it is especially effective if activated at the beginning of a Reiki Session. You can also use it at the end of a session to seal in the healing energy of Reiki.

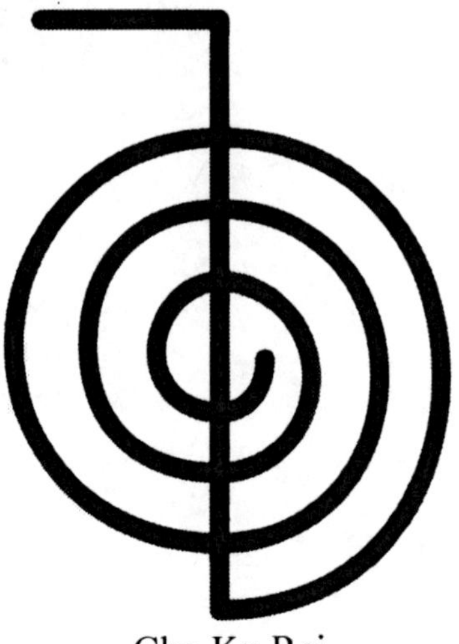

Cho Ku Rei

The Reiki Symbols that I use in this book are the symbols that are the truest to the traditional Usui lineage. Don't worry if the reiki symbols you were taught are slightly different from these. The symbols you received from your Reiki Master are the right symbols for you because you have been attuned to them.

If your symbols are different, and you feel you would like to be attuned to the Usui Reiki symbols used in this guide, you can attend one of my classes or find another Reiki Master that uses these symbols.

## How to Prepare for Your First Attunement.

There are several things that you can do to prepare your body and mind for the attunement. The first is to make sure your body is free of any food or drinks that might diminish your mental awareness or stimulate your body unnaturally.

These are things like cold and allergy medicines or food and drinks with excess refined sugar and caffeine. Try to avoid them for at least 24 hours prior to your class and drink plenty of water to flush out any toxins. Of course make sure you continue to take any prescription medicines according to your doctor's directions.

Go to bed early the night before your class so you get a full night's sleep. Don't stay up late watching television. It is also very important to a eat healthy, nutritious breakfast the day of your attunement.

Ten to 15 minutes of meditation exercises, like the ones you'll read about in Chapter 8, will help clear your mind and prepare your body emotionally and spiritually for the attunement.

## What You Do During Your Attunement

During the attunement you must sit quietly with your eyes closed. Closing your eyes helps you relax and achieve a meditative state. If you feel more comfortable with your eyes open, that's okay. But you should stare straight ahead and not look around during the attunement. You can focus your attention on a candle or crystal.

At certain points during the attunement you will need to move your hands to different positions. Your Reiki Master will either guide your hands to the position or tap your shoulder for you to move your hands to the next position. Here are the different hand positions and the order you will use them for your first attunement.

The first position is with your hands together in front of you. Your Reiki Master will begin the attunement process standing behind you.

First Position

Second Position

Your Reiki Master will remain behind you for the next hand position. For this one, you will keep your hands together and raise them above your head.

For the third hand position you will lower your hands in front of you, as in the first position, and open them with your palms facing up. Your Reiki Master will move to your front for this hand position.

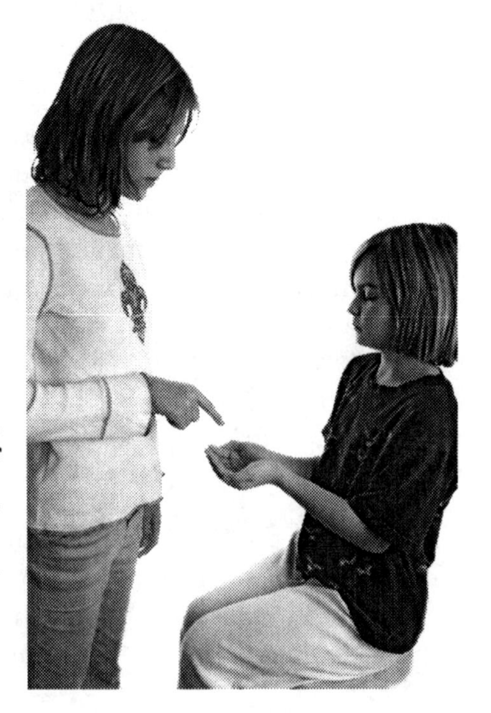

Third Position

## What to Expect During and After the Attunement

Most of the time people experience a physical reaction to the attunement or when they are using Reiki, or they my have a physical reaction after the session is over.

Most people like to have physical signs to show that Reiki is flowing during Reiki Attunements and during healing sessions. But sometimes people feel nothing at all. Don't worry, this does not mean the Reiki energy is not flowing.

The more you use Reiki, the easier it will be for you to sense when it is flowing into any body.

Some of the common physical reactions and sensations people have during and after Reiki Attunements are:

- Warm to very hot hands,
- Tingling sensations in hands or throughout the body,
- Hand cold to ice cold,
- Numbness in the hands and/or arms.

Some of the less common reactions are having visions, flashes of insight, out of body experiences, hear music, smells, and departed love ones or spirit guides might appear. Some people can just have a relaxed warm feeling all over.

You could experience many of these, just one, or none at all, or you could have your own unique experience or sensations that no one has had before.

Some people even have an emotional release from the Reiki Attunement and start to cry or their nose starts to run. This can happen when there is a release of old, deep rooted feelings and emotions.

All of these physical and emotional reactions are just part of the cleansing process. These experiences are harmless and you should not fear them. This is a releasing process that you must go through for healing. You are being opened to higher levels of consciousness and understanding.

After you complete your attunement, you are a Reiki Level One Practitioner. You can practice Reiki on yourself, your family, your plants, and even your pet!

# Chapter 4

# Healing Yourself With Reiki

*"The natural healing force within each one of us is the greatest force in getting well. . "*

- Hippocrates of Cos (460-377 BCE)
(Greek physician, Father of Medicine
and author of Oath of Medical Ethics)

There are many books and magazine articles that have documented Reiki healing, and even hospitals are starting to recognize the benefits of Reiki in the patients's healing process.

But Reiki is not magic, it's a healing modality. For example, if eating too much peanut butter gives you a stomach ache you can use Reiki to make the ache go away. But if you eat too much peanut butter again the stomach ache will return.

## Hand Positions for Healing Yourself

As a newly attuned Reiki Level One practitioner, you should follow a precise order of hand positions during each healing session and complete the entire sequence.

The twelve basic hand placements we use here give a full body Reiki treatment. There are four on the front of the body, four on the back of the body, and four on the head. Always begin with your face and move down the body in order to make sure you don't neglect any part of your body.

You should allow about five minutes at each position so that each area is given equal attention. As you go through each hand position, remember that you only need a gentle touch. Heavy pressure is not needed since you are working with energy exchange. You will see later that even touch is not required.

When you first start, it is a good idea to remove any rings or bracelets from your fingers and wrist. The vibrations and energy of gold, silver, or gemstones can affect the vibration you feel in your body.

After practicing the hand positions in this order for a period of time it is possible that you will feel the need to deviate from this pattern. You will begin to acquire your own methodology in placing your hands on your body by listening to your inner voice or intuition.

Before you begin you healing session, draw the Power Symbol three times in the palms of both of your hands. This will help increase the flow of Reiki. If you are Reiki Master, draw the Master Symbol three times in each palm after you draw the Power symbol.

Position 1

## Face

Hold the fingers and thumb of each hand together so there are no spaces between them, and then place the palms of your hands on your cheek bones.

Your hands should gently cup over your eyes with your finger tips gently against your forehead.

Position 2

## Top of the Head

Place the palms of your hands on either side of your head just above your ears. Your finger tips should meet at the top of your head.

Position 3

## Back of the Head

Place one hand on the back of your head just above the base of your skull, with the fingers pointing to the side. Place your other hand on your head just above the first hand.

Position 4

## Chin and Jaw

Place your hands together at the wrist and cup your chin in your hands. Your hand should extend along the jaw line so that your finger tips are gently resting on the ear lobes of each ear.

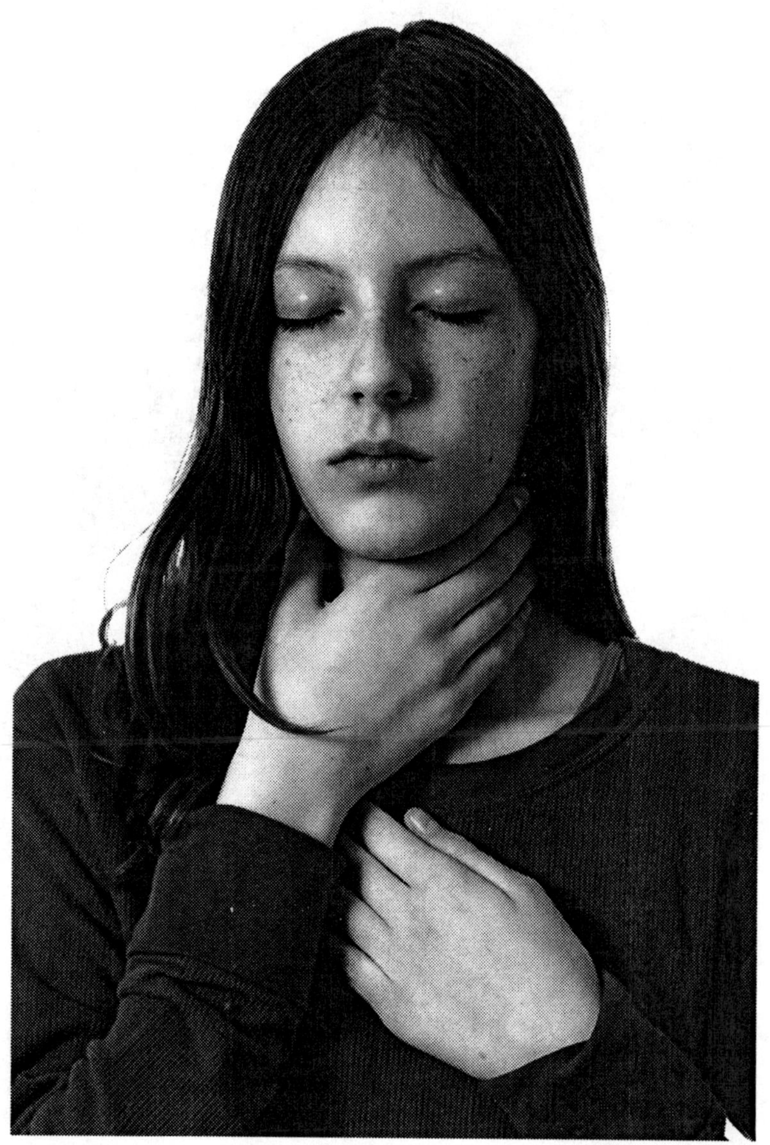

Position 5

## Throat and Heart

Place your right hand gently over your throat so that your thumb and index finger are touching the bottom of your jaw.

Place your left hand on the center of your chest between base of your neck and your heart.

Position 6

Ribs

Place your hands on your rib cage so that the finger tips are touching and your little fingers are on the bottom ribs.

Make sure your wrist are bent slightly so that your elbows are pointing backwards.

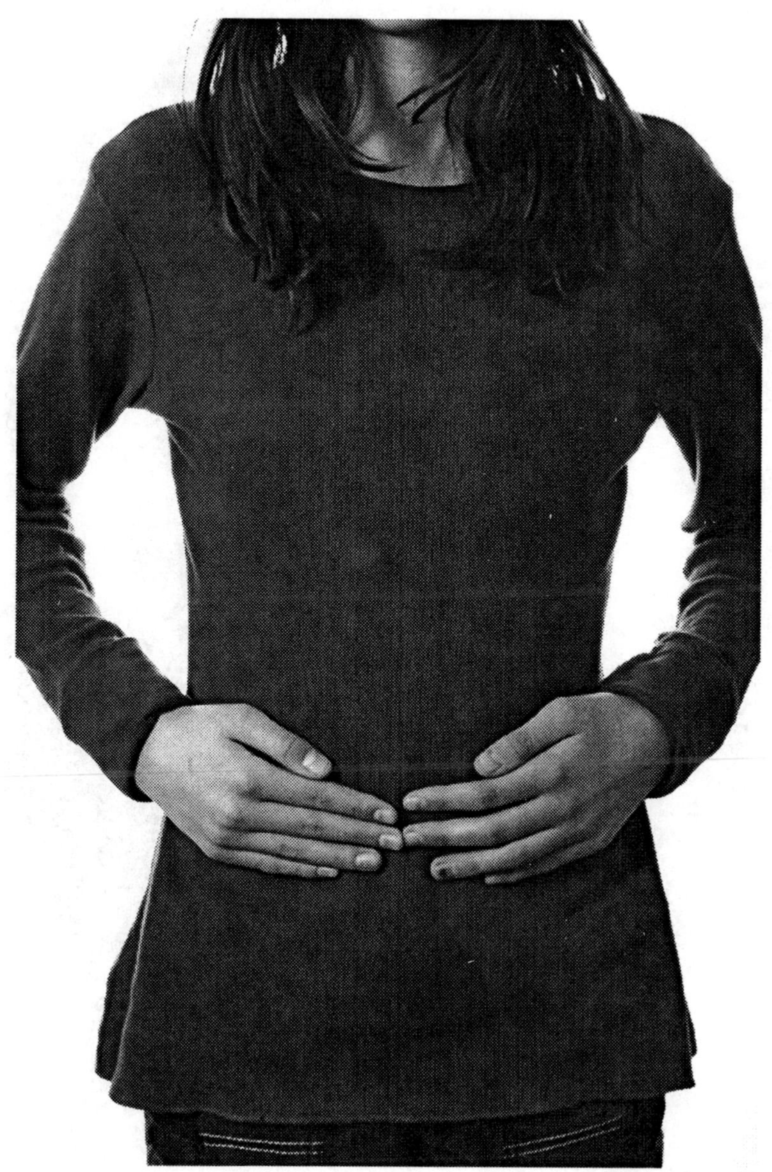

Position 7

## Abdomen

Place your hands below your rib cage so that the finger tips are touching and your thumbs are just touching the bottom ribs.

Make sure your wrist are bent slightly so that your elbows are pointing backwards.

Position 8

## Pelvic Bone

Place your right hand over the top of your right pelvic bone and your left hand over the top of your left pelvic bone so that the fingers tips of each hand are touching.

Make sure your wrist are bent slightly so that your elbows are pointing backwards.

Position 9

## Shoulders

Reach over the top of your shoulders with both hands and place them on your shoulder blades. If you can't reach your shoulder blades, reach as far as you can without stretching too hard. If you can't reach too far over your shoulders, you can place your hands on the top of each shoulder instead.

Position 10

## Mid Back

Place your hands on your back just below your rib cage so that the finger tips are touching.

If you can't reach far enough for your finger tips to touch, put them as close together as you can comfortably do so.

Position 11

## Lower Back

Place your hands on your back just above your hip bones so that the finger tips are touching.

If you can't reach far enough for your finger tips to touch, put them as close together as you can comfortably do so.

Position 12

## Sacrum

Place your hands on your sacral area with the palms of your hands resting on the top of the hip bones. Your fingers should be pointing inward and slightly downward.

# Chapter 5
# Healing Others With Reiki

*"Words have the power to both destroy and heal. When words are both true and kind, they can change our world."*

- Siddhartha Gautama
(Supreme Buddha, founder of Buddhism)

When you use Reiki on others, the Universal Life Force passes through you and into them. So you are also receiving Reiki when you help others.

The person receiving Reiki for healing can feel all of the same physical and emotional sensations as people do during Reiki attunements. Usually during a healing secession both the sender and receiver will have physical reactions. But you might not feel anything and the person receiving it will, or you might feel it and the person receiving the energy might have no reactions at all. The physical reactions and sensations of each Reiki session can be different.

## Scanning

Besides the hand positions, there is another important technique you can use in healing others. It's called scanning.

As you read in Chapter 3, the attunement process opens your palm chakras and allows you to channel Reiki energy through them to heal yourself and others. But you can also use your open palm chakra to detect problem areas in people and animals that need Reiki. Scanning is using your palm chakras to locate specific areas in the bodies that have problems and need extra Reiki.

Scanning works similar to the energy exercises that you practiced in Chapter 2. During scanning you go over the person's body, without touching them, to find changes in the energy in different areas of the body. The areas that "feel" different are the areas that need healing or need extra Reiki during a healing session. These imbalances could be illness that has not manifested in the body yet or they can be residual toxins from past illnesses.

A person may tell you that they have a specific problem; such their knee hurts, and asks you to channel Reiki to that area. But many times the area where they are having the problem is not what's causing their problem; it is only a symptom of something else. By scanning you can find the area that is the true cause of the problem and you can find areas that need healing before they get serious.

You can think of it like this. Your mom asks you to dry the floor because it is wet. You dry it, but in a few days the floor is wet again. You fixed the symptom by drying the floor but you didn't fix the problem. The roof of the house is leaking water on the floor and until you fix the roof, the floor will get wet again and again.

So, if someone says their knee is hurting it could be just the knee, or it could be that they fell down and bruised their hip and now when they walk, more stress is on that knee. You just don't know. But the body knows and it will tell you! Unless you heal the root cause of the pain, the knee will start to hurt once the stress from the hips builds up again.

## What to expect in Scanning

Have the person you are scanning lay down. They can sit in a chair but this will make the scanning process a little more difficult.

Before you start scanning you should draw the Power Symbol in the palms of both your hands. If you are a Reiki Master you should also draw the Master Symbol.

You can scan with one or both of your hands. Starting at the person's head place your hands about 3-6 inched above their body. Slowly move your palms over the body. As you do you will sense how the person energy feels. Stop over any areas that you feel there is as change in the energy. This is where the body needs Reiki.

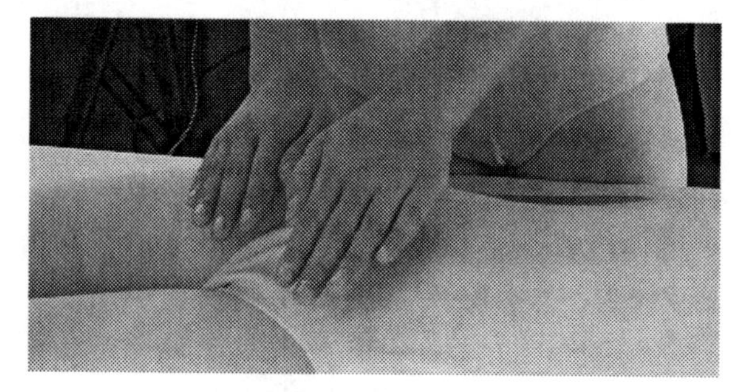

Scanning the body

You can feel a change in energy in many different ways. Some of the sensations you may feeling include:

- Warm heat slightly higher than body temperature
- Strong, more intense heat.
- Tingling sensation or ache in the fingers or hands
- Cold sensation
- Lack of energy
- Pulse-like or throbbing sensation in your hands
- Pins and needles in your hands
- Magnetic pull or pushing in your hands
- A strange vibration
- Pain in the palms of the hands

The more intense the feeling or pain is, the longer it will take to bring the area back to balance with the rest of the body. In some situations you may feel the pain in the back of your hands, your wrist, and even all the way to your elbows. Don't worry if you feel pain. You can't receive any of the negative energy from the person. This not anything that you should be afraid of, it is simply the way the body tells you where it needs Reiki.

Channel Reiki into the area where you felt the change in energy until the sensation goes away and you feel that the area is balanced with the rest of the person's energy.

If you are feeling pain and it becomes to much for you, you can take your hands off the person for a short time. Gently shake-out your hands and allow your pain to stop. When you feel ready, you can start channeling energy again. Do this as many times as you need until the pain is gone and you feel the area is balanced with the rest of the body.

Once the area is balanced, continue your scan down the body. Stop if you find other areas that are not in balance or feel different and channel Reiki until they are in balance again. Once you have reach the person's feet, have them turn over and repeat the process starting at the feet working your way up to the person's head.

The amount of time needed for a scanning session will depend on how many areas you find that need Reiki.

This process can find problems in all four of our bodies: the mental, physical, emotional and spiritual.

Just as with the energy exercises, the more you practice scanning, the more sensitive your palm chakras will be become and the easier it is for you to find the areas that need healing. This is a slow learning process that will grow as you give Reiki to others.

This is the healing technique that was used before the hand positions were developed.

## Hand Positions for Healing

Although Reiki can be used intuitively, here are some of the hand positions you can use to heal different parts of the body until you develop your sensitivity to the subtle changes in a person's energy.

The hand placement for giving Reiki treatments to others as similar to those used when performing self-healing. These positions will help you focus your intention during the healing sessions.

You should allow 3 to 5 minutes per hand position. A full body treatment will normally last 60 to 90 minutes. However, the hand positions are just guidelines until you develop your sensitivity enough to work intuitively. The amount of time you stay on each area will change as you learn to feel when those areas become balanced.

Before you begin your healing session, draw the Power Symbol three times in the palms of both of your hands. If you are a Reiki Master, draw the Master Symbol three times in each palm after you draw the Power symbol.

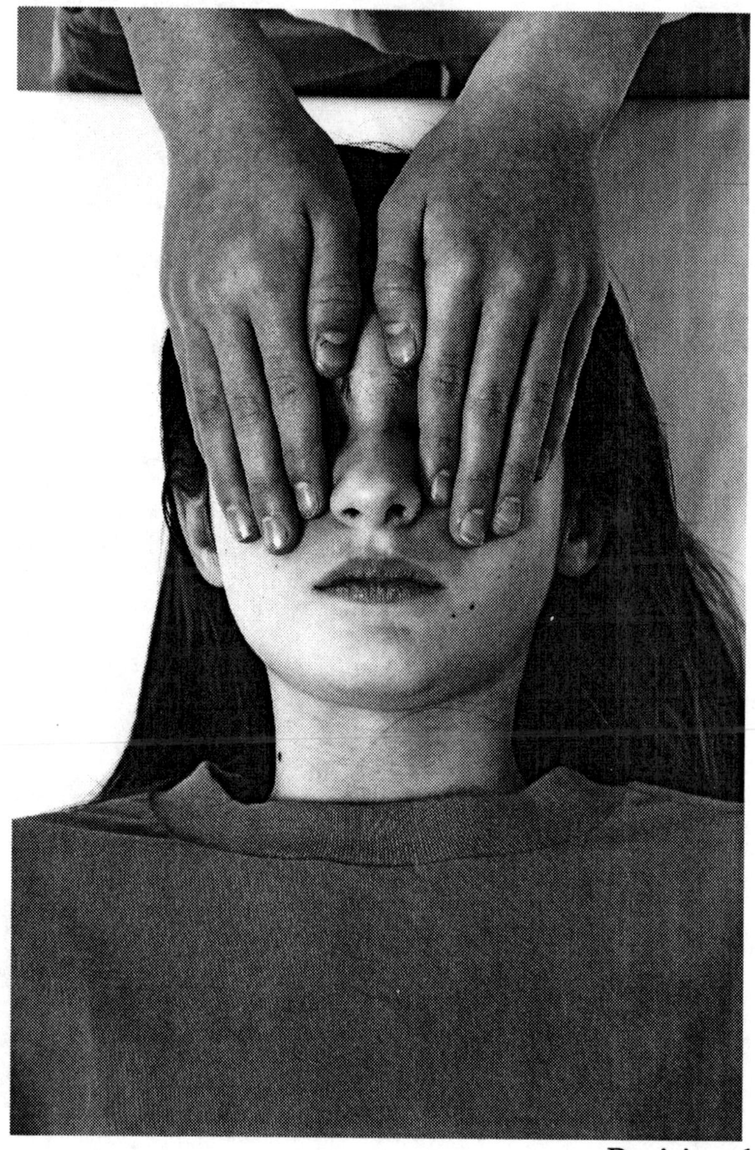

Position 1

## Face

Hold the fingers and thumb of each hand together so there are no spaces between them, and then gently cup your fingers over the eyes with your palms gently against the forehead. This position is related to the 6th chakra and helps with the eyes, ears, nose, nervous system and pituitary gland.

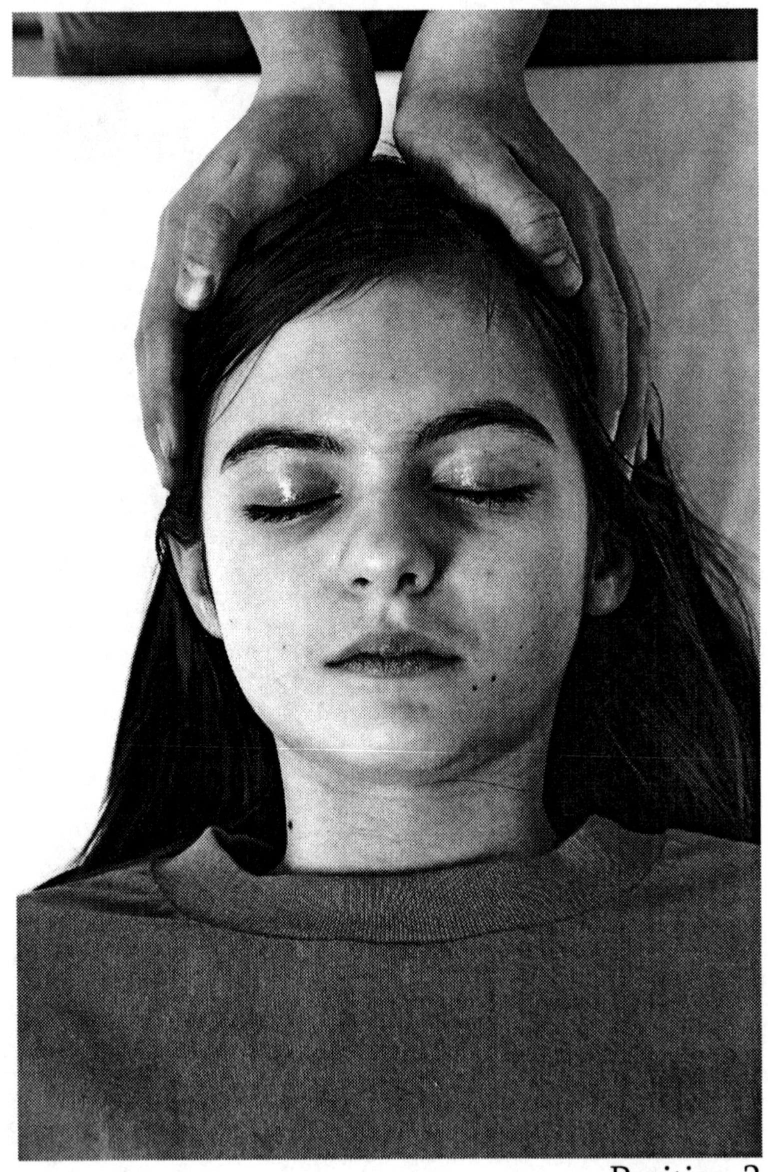

Position 2

## Crown and Top of the Head

With the inner wrist of your hand touching, place the base of your palms on the top of the head at the crown. Your hands should wrap around the head with your finger tips touching the tops of the ears. This position relates to the 7th chakra and treats the brain and pineal gland.

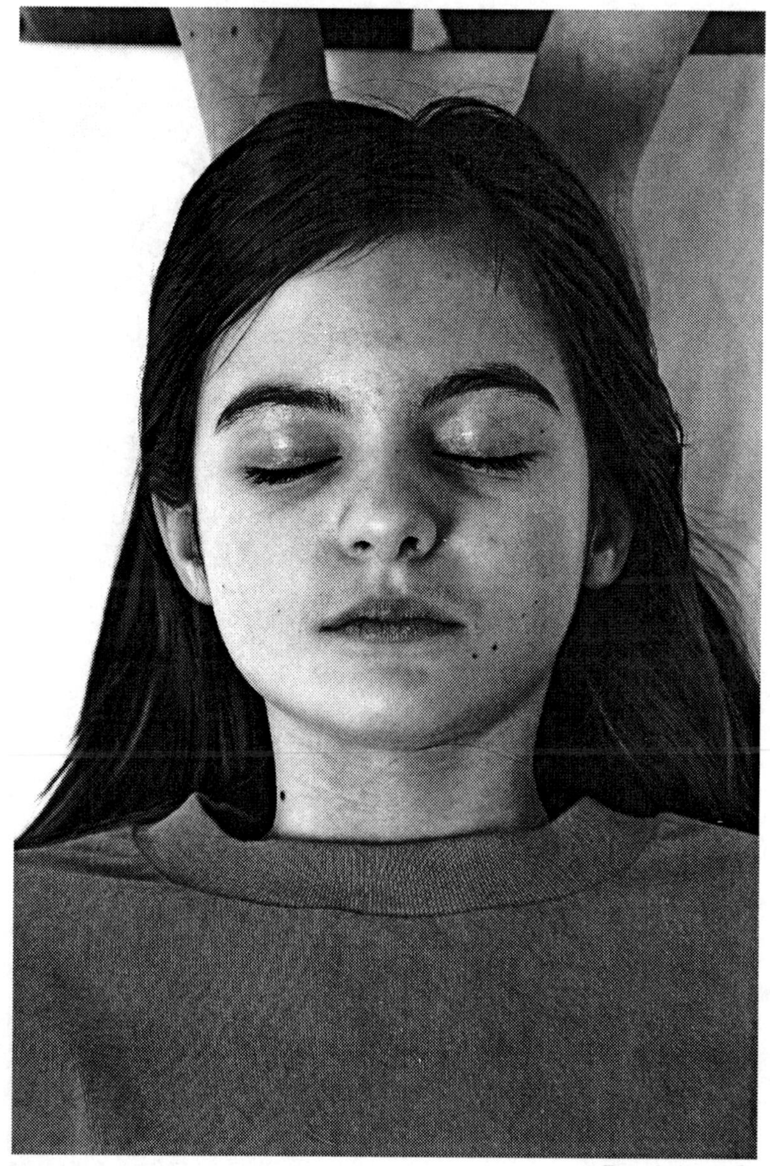

Position 3

## Back of the Head

Gently place the palms of your hands under the head as a cradle with your fingers pointing toward the neck. Allow your hands to rest on the table. This position is related to the 6th chakra and treats the back of the head.

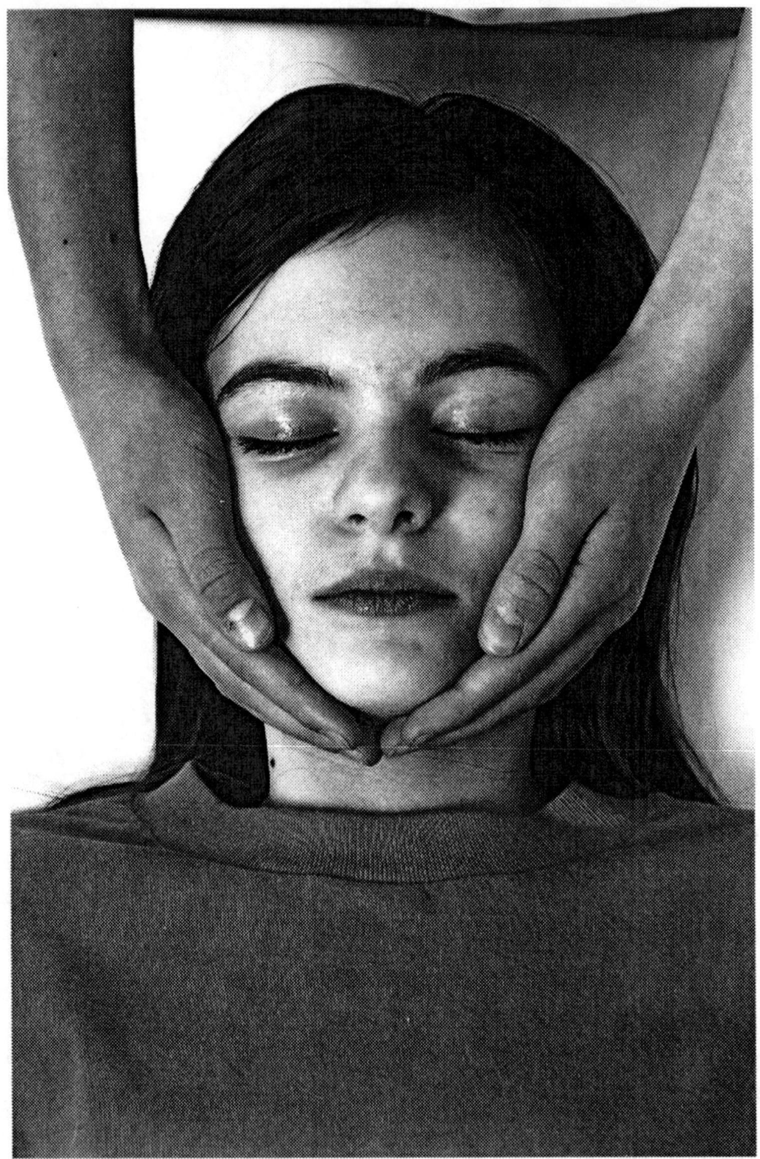

Position 4

## Chin and Jaw Line

Place your hands under the chin along the jaw line. Your finger tips should touch under the chin. This position is related to the 5th chakra and helps to treat thyroid and parathyroid glands, vocal cords, larynx and lymph nodes.

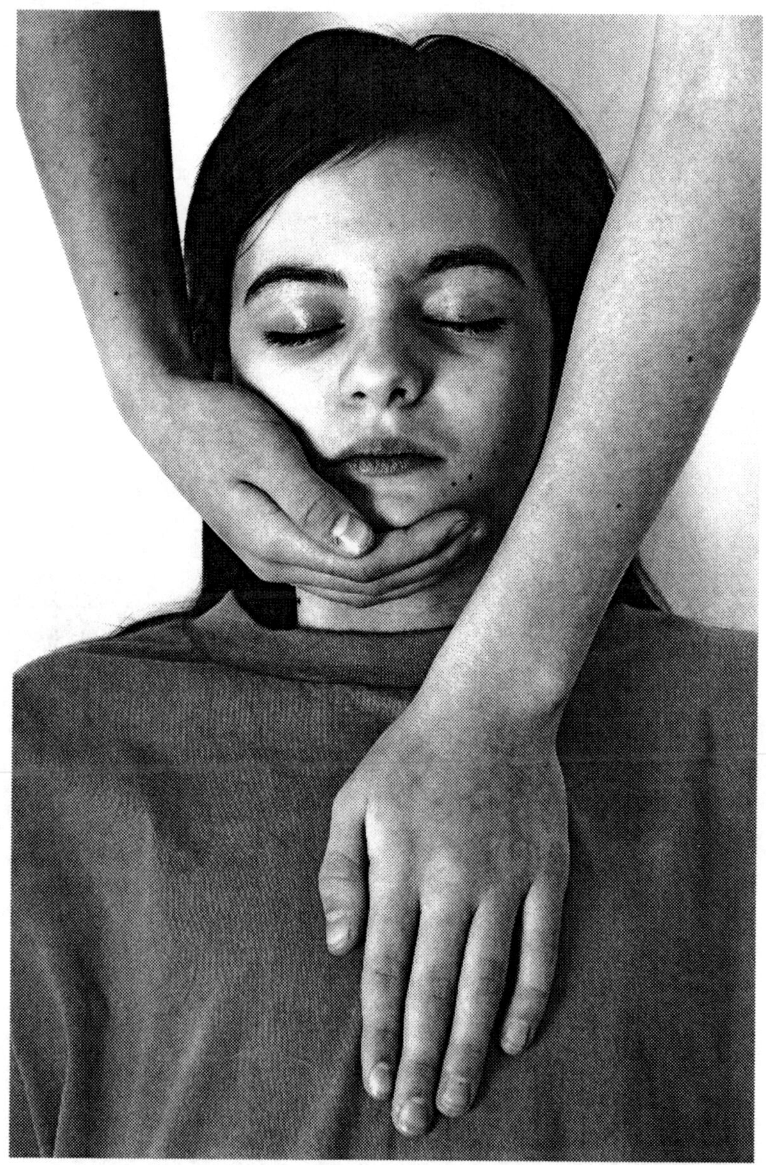

Position 5

## Neck, Collarbone, and Heart

Place your right hand under the chin along the jaw line so that the chin is cradled in your hand. Place your left hand over the heart with your fingers pointed downward. This position is related to the 4th and 5th chakra and helps with the circulatory system, breast and thymus gland.

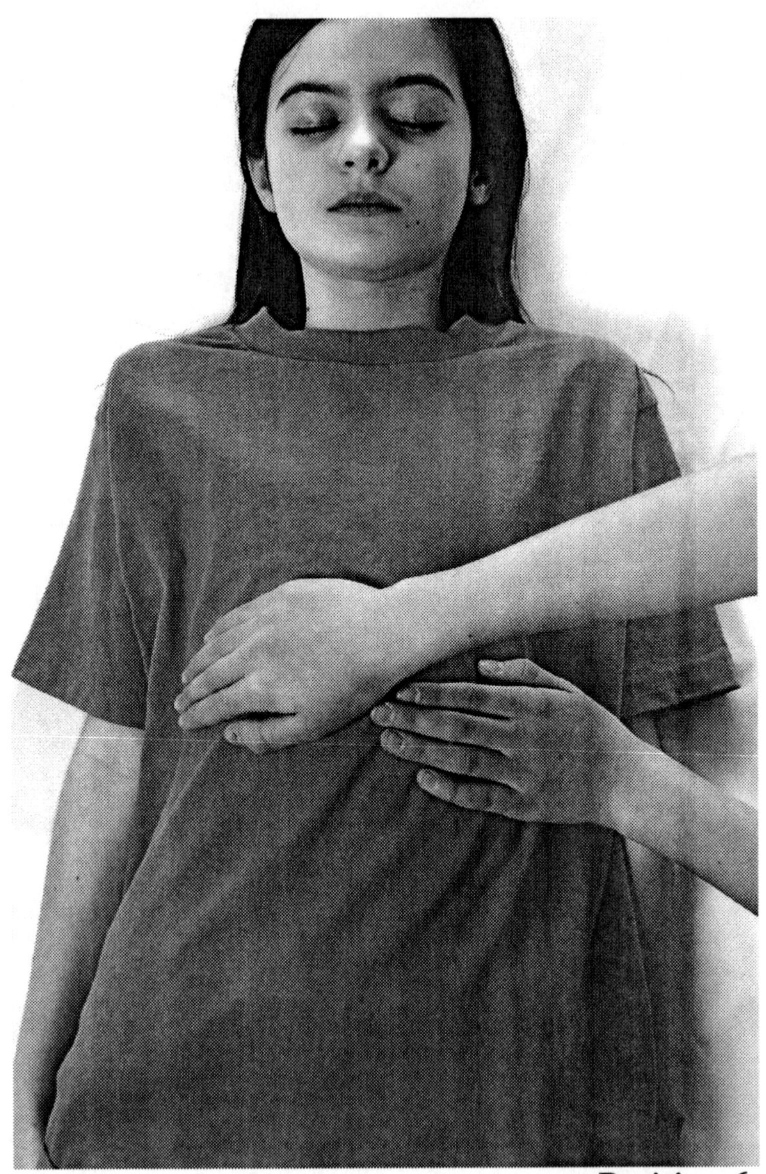

Position 6

## Ribs or Upper Abdomen

Place hands across the ribs. This position is related to the 3rd chakra and helps treat the liver, spleen, digestive tract and pancreas.

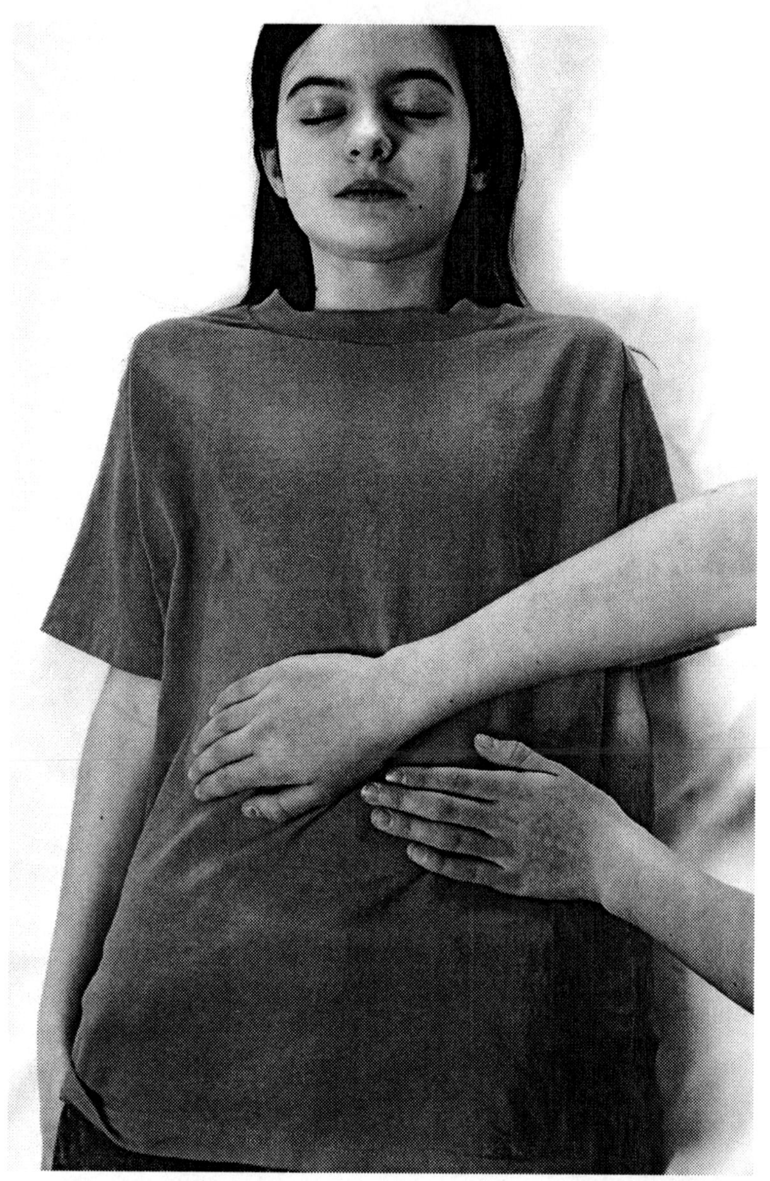

Position 7

## Abdomen

Place your hand across the solar plexus just above the belly button. This position helps treat the gallbladder, pancreas, and large and small intestines.

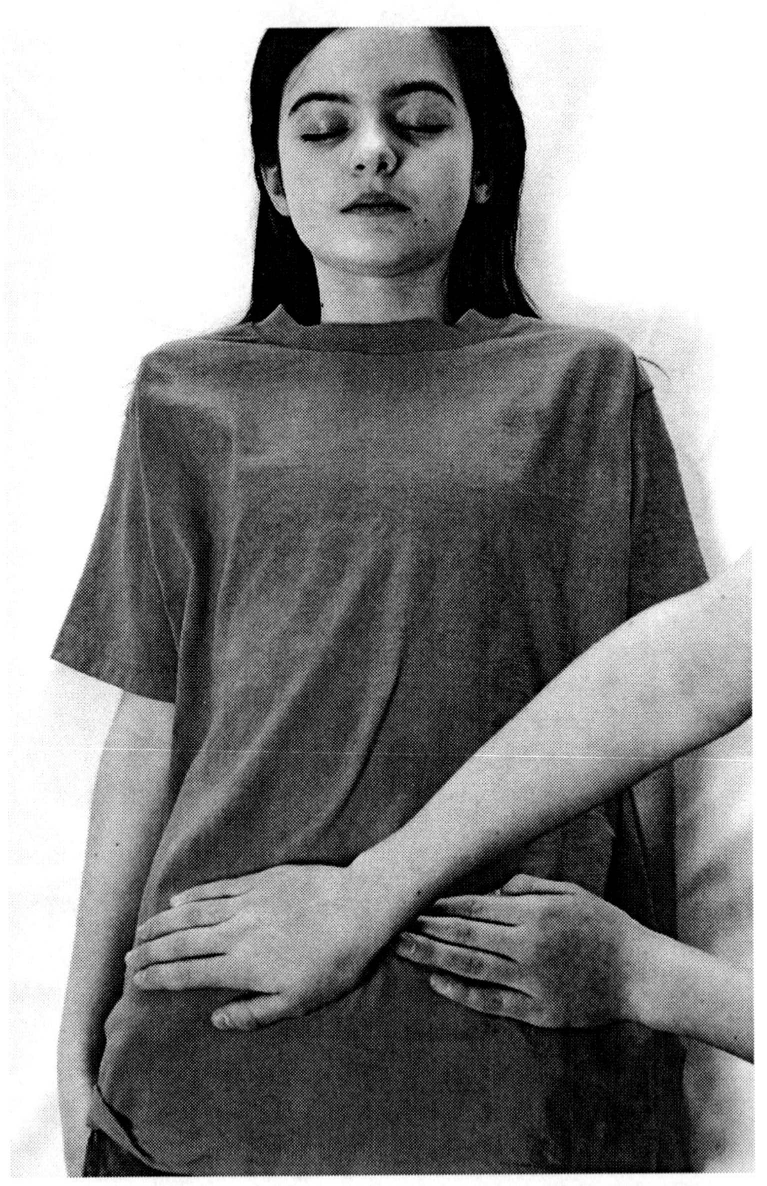

Position 8

## Pelvic Bone or Lower Abdomen

Place your hands on the lower stomach, just over the pelvic bones. This position is related to the 2nd chakra and helps send energy to your bladder, reproductive organs and your large and small intestines.

Position 9

## Shoulder Blades

Place your hand over both shoulder blades. This position helps relieve tension of the neck and shoulders.

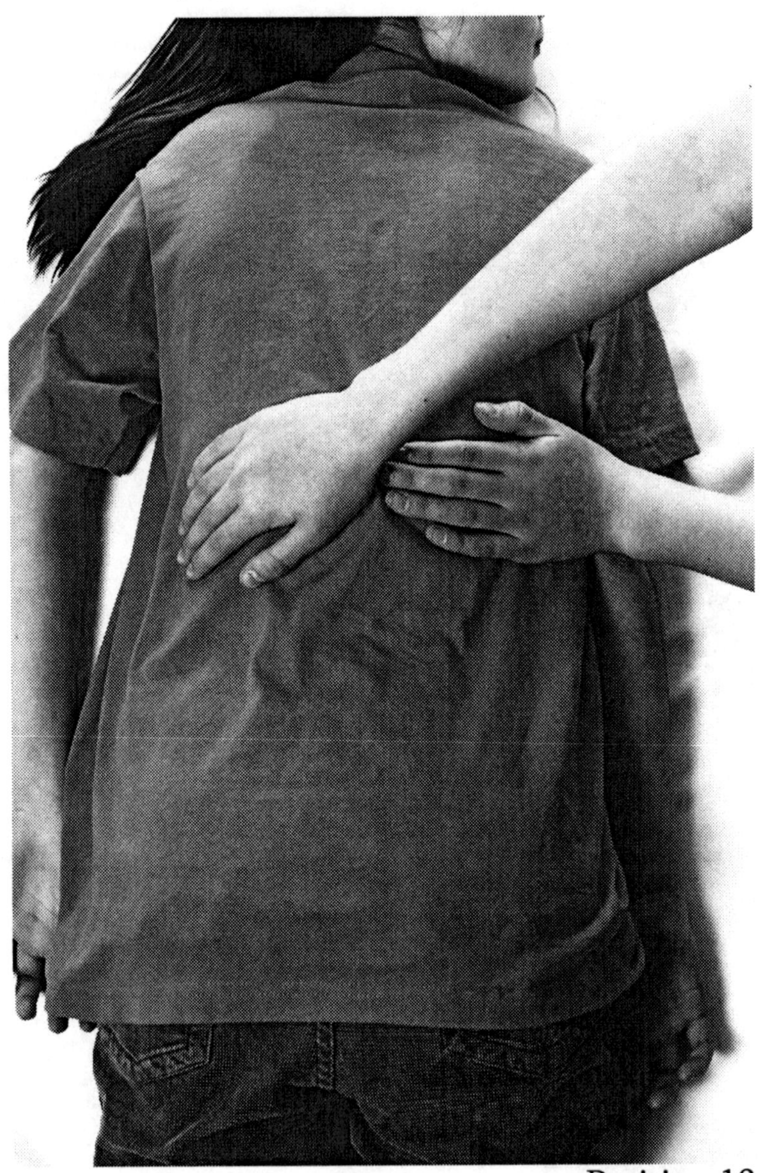

Position 10

## Mid Back

Place your hands across the middle of the back just below the shoulder blades. This position is related to the 4th chakra and treats the heart and lungs.

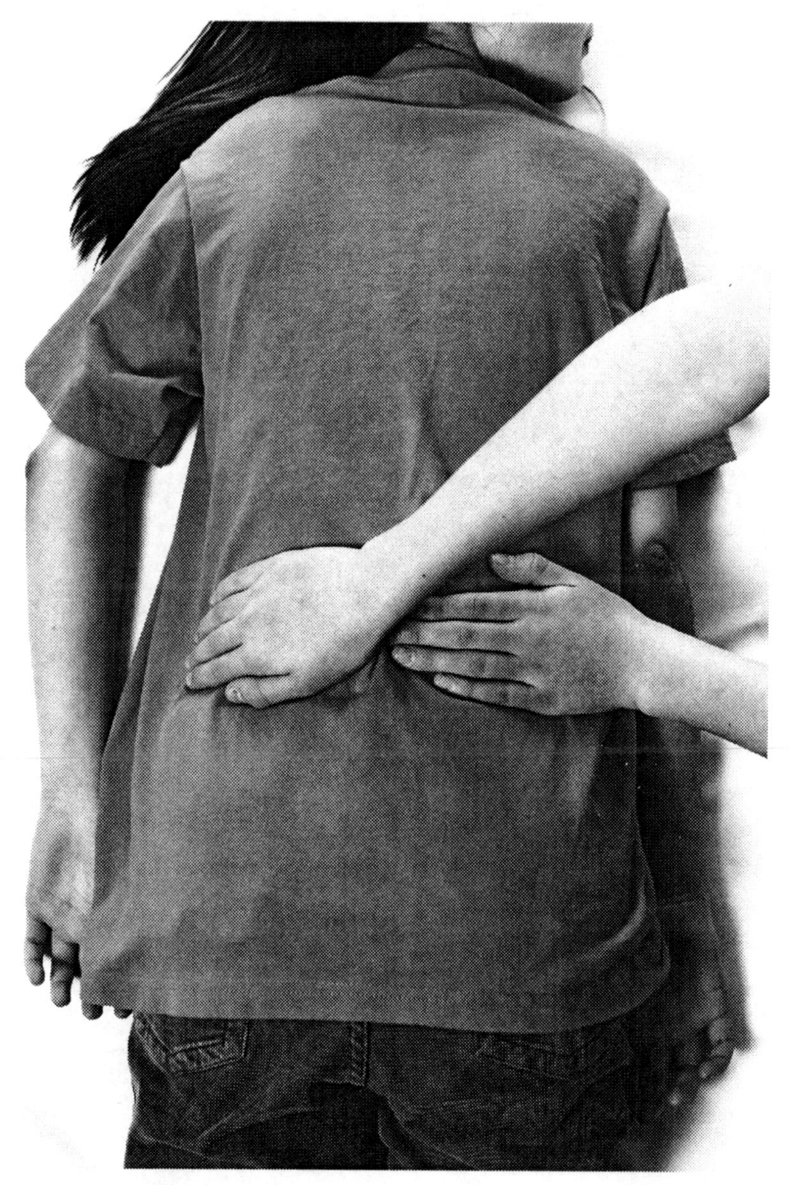

Position 11

## Lower Back or Waist

Place your hands across the lower back on the waist area. This position is related to the 3rd chakra and helps treat the adrenal glands and the kidneys.

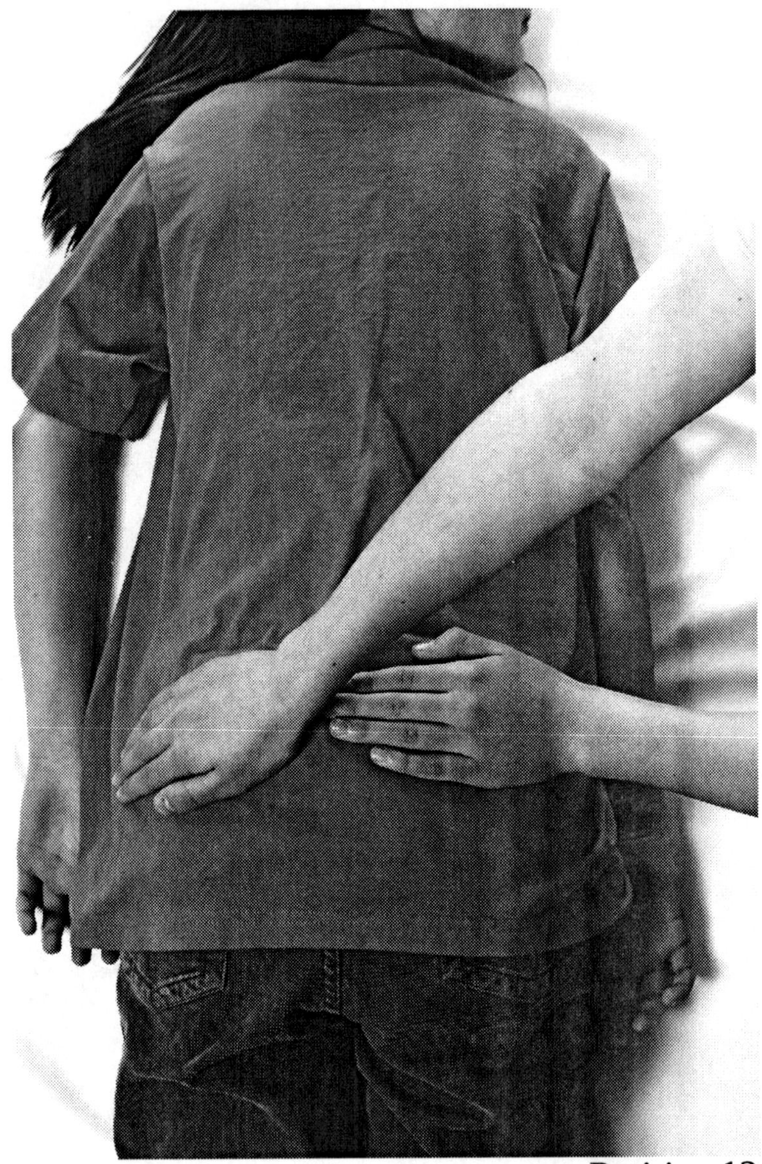

Position 12

Sacrum

Place your hands across the sacrum region or the hollow of the lower back. It is related to the 2nd chakra and helps release tension.

# Chapter 6
# Reiki Attunement Level Two

*"Oh, the powers of nature! She knows what we need, and the doctors know nothing."*

Benvenuto Cellini (1500-1571)
(Italian goldsmith, painter, sculptor, soldier and musician of the Renaissance.)

Level Two Reiki Attunement is a continuation of level one and you must be attuned as level one before you can begin level two training. This attunement works more directly on the spiritual body and stimulates growth and development on your intuitiveness.

For level two, you will also learn two more Reiki symbols. They are the Mental/Emotional Symbols and the Distant Healing Symbol.

## Sei Hei Ki

During your Second Level Attunement the Mental-Emotional symbol is used to help increase your intuitiveness and promote balance. The Japanese name for this symbol is Sei Hei Ki. (pronounced say hay key)

Sei Hei Ki's meaning is "God and humanity become one." Every time you draw this symbol you bring more balance in life.

Sei Hei Ki

Sei Hei Ki symbol can be used to heal psychological and emotional problems, to increase love and forgiveness of yourself and in relationships, or to change habits and heal additions.

When using this symbol, you activate it with your intention for what you want it to do. If you are helping someone stop smoking, the intent would be to help break the addiction and habit of smoking.

## Hon Sha Ze Sho Nen

The Distance Symbol helps to remove the illusion of time and space and brings a unity of all beings. The Japanese name for this symbol is Hon Sha Ze Sho Nen. (pronounced hahn shah zey show nen)

Hon Sha Ze Sho Nen

The name Hon Sha Ze Sho Nen is translated several different ways, but I was taught that is means "the origin of all is pure consciousness."

Hon Sha Ze Sho Nen symbol is used to heal someone that is not in the same location as you. In other words, distant healing. (see Chapter 7)

You use the Distance Symbol at the beginning of your Reiki session any time you are giving Reiki at a distance or to connect your higher self or the higher self of others.

## How to Prepare for Your Second Attunement.

You should prepare for your Level Two Attunement just as you did for your Level One Attunement.

The first, make sure your body is free of any food or drinks that might diminish your mental awareness or stimulate your body unnaturally. These are things like cold and allergy medicines or food and drinks with excess refined sugar and caffeine. Try to avoid them for at least 24 hours prior to your class and drink plenty of water to flush out any toxins. Of course make sure you continue to take any prescription medicines according to your doctor's directions.

Don't stay up late watching television and make sure you get a full night's sleep the night before, and eat a nutritious breakfast the day of your attunement.

Ten to 15 minutes of meditation exercises, like the ones you'll read about in Chapter 8, will help clear your mind and prepare your body emotionally and spiritually for the attunement.

## What You Do During Your Second Attunement

Just as with your first attunement, you must sit quietly with your eyes closed, or if you feel more comfortable with your eyes open, you should stare straight ahead and not look around during the attunement. You can focus your attention on a candle or crystal.

At certain points during the attunement you will need to move your hands to different positions just like the first time and the order is the same as in your first attunement. (see Chapter 3) The only difference is what your Reiki Master does at the beginning and end of the attunement process.

Before you move your hands to the first position, your Reiki Master will stand behind you with their hands on the top of your head for 15 to 30 second. This is to help start the energy connection. At the end of the attunement, your Reiki Master will stand behind you again and place their hands on your shoulders for a few seconds, and then bring their hands up so that their thumbs are on the back of your neck touching the base of your skull.

After you complete your attunement, you are a Reiki Level Two Practitioner. You can practice Reiki to help with emotional and psychological problems and perform distance healing!

# Chapter 7
# Distant Healing

*"The art of healing comes from nature, not from the physician. Therefore the physician must start from nature, with an open mind."*

- Philipus Aureolus Paracelsus (1493 - 1541)
(Swiss-born alchemist & physician)

In the previous chapters you've learn how to give Reiki to yourself and to others, but what if someone you know needs Reiki but they are not with you? What if they live in another city, state or even another country? You can still send Reiki to that person by using distant healing techniques.

Distant Reiki is referred to by several different names such as long-distance Reiki, remote healing, distance healing, healing in absentia, and non-local healing, but the techniques used are basically the same.

Distant Reiki techniques are taught as part of Level Two Reiki training and the third Reiki symbol that you learn is called the Distance Symbol or the Connection Symbol. The use of this symbol allows you to send Reiki energy to anyone, anywhere, at anytime.

## Distant Reiki Technique

First find a quiet location where you will not be disturbed. Sit down and make sure you are comfortable and relaxed. If you need help in relaxing and clearing your mind, you can practice meditation prior to starting the distant healing session. (see Chapter 8)

Step 1. Visualize and say the names of the Distant Symbol, the Emotional Symbol and then the Power Symbol three times each. Saying the names of the symbols three times makes the symbol a mantra, bringing you the energy associated with the symbol.

Hon Sha Ze Sho Nen (Distant)
Hon Sha Ze Sho Nen
Hon Sha Ze Sho Nen

Sei Hei Ki (Emotional)
Sei Hei Ki
Sei Hei Ki

Cho Ku Rei (Power)
Cho Ku Rei
Cho Ku Rei

Step 2. Visualize or picture the person in your mind and set your intention to send Reiki to that person by saying the person's name three times.

Step 3. Visualize and say the names of Distant Symbol, the Emotional Symbol and then the Power Symbol three times each (just as in step 1)

Step 4. Draw the Power symbol and the Master Symbol (if you are attuned to the master symbol) in the palms of both of your hands three times each.

Step 5. Perform aura clearing (see Chapter 8)

Step 6. Scan the person just as you would in person (see Chapter 5)

Step 7. Perform your healing session just as you would in person. If you are still new to Reiki and developing your intuition, you should use the hand positions. (see Chapter 5)

Step 8. End the session with an aura clearing.

Just as different teachers may draw the symbols slightly different, you may find different distant healing techniques with each Reiki practitioner.

## Using a Substitute

If you have a hard time visualizing the person during distant healing you can use a surrogate or a substitute for the person. You can use a photograph of the person or even a stuffed toy animal or doll.

To use the substitute, place it in front of you before you begin the distant healing session. When you get to step 2, look at the picture or doll and pretend that it is the person in front of you. Say the person name three times.

You can scan and perform all the healing techniques to the substitute just as if the person was there with you. Your intention will send the Reiki to where ever the person might be.

# Chapter 8
# Enhancing Your Energy

*"Let Om be the bow, mind the arrow, and Higher Consciousness the target. Those who want enlightenment should reflect on the sound and the meaning of Om. When the arrow is released from the bow it goes straight to the target."*

- Dhyana Bindu Upanishad*

Even though you channel the universal life force to the person you are healing, and not your personal energy, the closeness required during a Reiki treatment session can result in your energy interacting with the person's energy you are treating.

So the more relaxed and calmer you are when you start your healing session, better the experience for the other person. And the more focused you are in setting your intentions to heal, the more effective the treatment will be.

This chapter will provide you with several exercises and techniques to help ground you before you channel Reiki and increase the effectiveness

**The Upanishad are spiritual interpretation of the Vedas, which are the most ancient books in the World, and are the foundation of Hinduism. The Dhyana Bindu is the mediation on the sound of Om, or the Primordial Vibration.*

of your healing sessions.

## Simple Meditation

Meditation is the act of calming your mind and body. Closing our eyes and thinking of something really good is a kind of meditation. Before you practice your Reiki you might want to meditate to help you better focus and use your healing powers.

Here is a basic meditation you can practice. It is called the Tree of Life meditation.

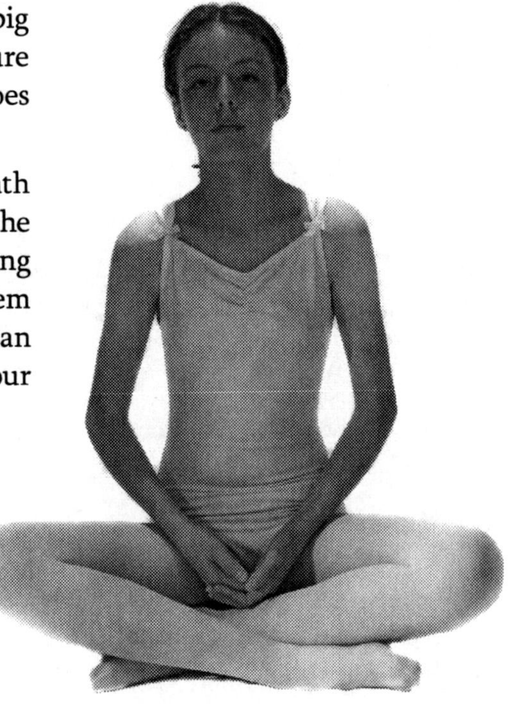

Imagine you are a tree, take a big breath and as you exhale picture your roots growing out of your toes and down into the earth.

Now take another deep breath and as you exhale, picture the branches of your tree sprouting out the top of your head. Feel them reach toward the warm sun. Can you feel the sun warm against your leaves?

Now take another deep breath and breathe in the rays of the sun, as you exhale feel the warmth of the sun as it moves down through your body and back into the earth.

Repeat this mental exercise three times beginning with extending your roots into the earth. This will strengthen your connection with the earth and give you more energy for your healing.

## Mantras

In Chapter Two you learned that all living things have vibrations and that those vibrations can have good or bad effects on you. When you hear sounds you are actually hearing vibrations. The vibrations that create sounds can also have powerful effects on you. The sound of rainfall or birds singing can have a soothing and calming effect on you, but hearing fingernails scratching across a chalkboard can have the opposite result. When you speak you create vibrations with your vocal cords and mouth that people can hear. The vibrations of some words can have a direct physical and emotional affects on you. Mantras are words or short phrases used to create soothing sounds that connect you to your higher self and to the collective consciousness of the universe.

Mantra is created from the two Sanskrit words of manas and trai. "Manas" means "mind," and "trai" means to "protect" or "free from" so the meaning of Mantra is "to set free from the mind." Hymns, prayers, ritualistic incantations or verbal spells are considered the same as a mantras. These short phrases are used in all religions of the world to create changes in consciousness and to bring practitioners closer to their divine being, creator, or closer to nature.

There are hundreds of Mantras and each corresponds to a specific spiritual energy vibration and to a specific desired state of mind. When you use Mantras they start a powerful vibration that causes changes in your body and mind. Over time, the mantra process begins to override other vibrations and creates a harmonic resonance, where your entire being vibrates at the same rate as the mantra. This brings you completely in tune or in harmony with the energy and spiritual state of the specific mantra.

Mantras can give us the power to: cure diseases, ward off evil, gain wealth, acquire supernatural powers, attain a blissful state, and many other purposes.

## Om

We will use the simple but very powerful Mantra of Om to help increase our healing energy and to focus us on the healing process. The mantra Om was handed down to us by ancient Himalayan sages and is the most important Mantra. Almost all of the other Mantras begin and even end with Om. Om is of great importance in the religion of Hinduism and represents the source of all things in existence. Elements of Om can be found in many other cultures and religions such as Judaism, Christianity, Islam, Jainism, Sikhism and Buddhism. There is also evidence that Om was used in ancient Egypt and by the Celts.

You should not think about Om as just a simple word but instead as an intonation, or chant, that transcends age, race, culture and even species. This simple mantra harmonizes your physical, emotional, and intellectual aspects of who you are. Om completely changes the way you understand those things around you, within you, and beyond you.

Om is made up of three Sanskrit letters, aa, au and ma which, when combined together, make the sound "AUM'. The following exercises will show you how to say and use this simple yet powerful mantra.

## Exercise 1: Saying Om

The "A" sound is pronounced "AH" as in "father" and should resonate in the center of your mouth. The "U" sound is pronounced as the ending in the word "who" and transfers the vibration to the back of your mouth. The third sound of "M" is just humming with your lips gently closed. This sound should resonate at the front of your mouth and vibrate throughout your head. Try saying Om (Aum) several times before doing the exercise below.

## Exercise 2: Feeling Om

1. Start in the standing position with your feet shoulder width apart with your hands and arms hanging comfortably at your sides.

2. Inhale gently and easily while you expand your breath into your belly and prepare to make all three vowels of the "AUM" sound in one seamless breath. You should create the intention of sound of the "A" before you actually make the sound by opening your mouth as you inhale and visualize that you are inhaling the "A" sound itself.

3. As you begin to make the "A" sound, slowly raise your arms straight out to your side as if you are trying embrace the entire universe.

Step 3: Open to Embrace the Energy of the Universe

Here you are connecting with the infinite energy of the universe and the energy of unity of consciousness.

Step 4: Build the Energy

4. As you start to change the sound from the "A" to "U" extend your arms to your front and visualize your reiki energy building between your hands (like the exercise in Chapter Two). Here you are bringing the energy of the universe to your reality or plane of existents where you can feel and use it.

Step 5: Absorb the Energy

5. As the "U" turns into to the "M" sound, bring your hands and the energy they contain to about 3 inches about your Heart Chakra. Here you are absorbing that energy into your own body.

6. Then, as the "M" sound fades, gently place your palms on your chest

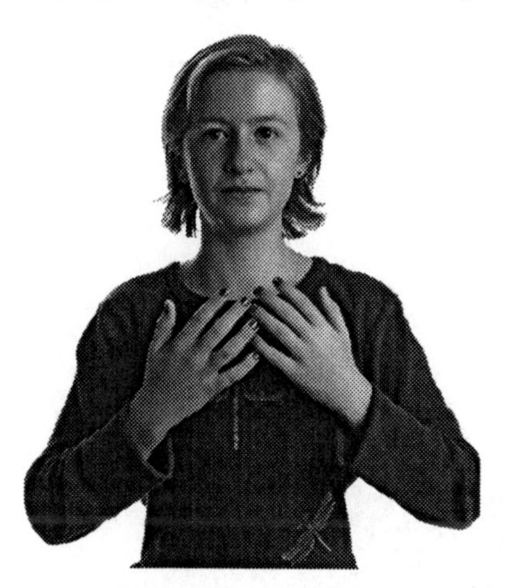

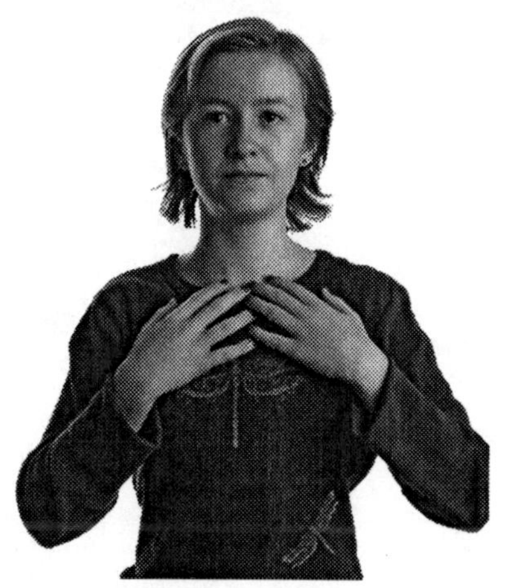

Step 6: Place the Energy in Your Heart and Let it Resonate Within You

placing the energy lovingly into your heart. Breathe gently. Here you are allowing the energy to resonate within you.

7. Slowly repeat steps 3, 4, 5 and 6 several times allowing these steps to take 4 to 5 seconds to complete.

Do these exercises before each Reiki session to relax and center you and to help you mentally set your focus on the healing process.

## Aura Clearing and Protection

By clearing the aura before you begin the healing session, you clear away some of the stagnant or negative energy from the person making it easier for the person to receive the Reiki energy.

After the Reiki session is complete, clearing the aura helps maintain the balance and protects the aura from picking up more stagnant or negative energy

To perform an aura clearing,

1. Have the person lie down in a comfortable position

2. Place your hands 3-6 inches above the top of the person's head

3. Using one continuous sweeping motion, move your hands from the top of the person's head to below the feet. Keep your hands 3-6 inches above the person's body during the entire sweep.

4. Return your hands to the top of the head do two more sweeps.

# Chapter 9
# Master Attunement

*"The best way to find yourself is to lose yourself in the service of others."*

- Mahatma Gandhi (1869-1948)
(India's "Father of the Nation")

Years ago it was normal for a Level Two practitioner to wait for 3-10 years before they were allowed to receive the Master Level Attunement. Now it is not uncommon for Reiki Level One and Level Two given on back-to-back in one weekend, and Master Level given when the student feels he is ready.

I feel it is important for the you to study all aspects of Reiki and practice for at least 6 months before considering training for Master Level. The reason for waiting is to give you time to integrate your Reiki experiences so that you're better prepared for the master level training.

When you make the decision to advance to Master Level, it is very important for you ask what type of training you will receive in the class before you sign-up.

As we discussed in Chapter 3, traditionally there is only three levels of Reiki. However some branches and schools of Reiki divided the Master Level in to two classes. These classes are usually referred to as Level IIIa and Level IIIb or as Advanced Reiki Techniques (ART) and Master Level.

Unfortunately, dividing the Master Level into two separate classes or levels, has created some confusion in the use of titles associated with the training. You may hear the titles of: Reiki Level Three Practitioner, Reiki Master and Reiki Master/Teacher, or variations of these three titles.

In some cases the title of Reiki Master is used by all three methods. Here are the basic distinctions between the titles and what they mean:

Reiki Level Three Practitioner

A Reiki Level Three Practitioner is a practitioner who received the Reiki Master level attunement but were not shown or taught the master symbol.

Reiki Master

A Reiki Master is a practitioner who received the Reiki Master level attunement and was taught the Master Symbol.

Reiki Master/Teacher

A Reiki Master/Teacher is a Reiki practitioner who received a Reiki Master level attunement, was taught the Master Symbol and how to teach Reiki classes and perform attunements to others.

Graduation from a Reiki master level class does not end your learning in Reiki. As you continue to use Reiki and teach others Reiki you will continue to learn more and more about Reiki. Reiki will become integrated is every aspect of your life.

A true master of any art or craft understands that becoming a master is about mastering yourself.

# STYLES OF REIKI

There are many different styles of Reiki that have develpoped since Mikao Usui created Usui Reiki Ryoho. Here is a list of just some of the sytles found throughout the world.

Angel Touch Reiki
Anugraha Reiki
Ascension Reiki
Authentic Reiki
Blue Star Reiki
Brahma Satya Reiki
Buddho Ennersense Reiki
Gakkai Reiki
Gendai Reiki
Golden Age Reiki
Ichi Sekai Reiki
Imara Reiki
Innersun Reiki
Japanese Reiki
Jikiden Reiki
Jinlap Maitre Reiki
Johrei Reiki
Kava Reiki
Karuna Ki
Karuna Reiki
Ken Reiki-do
Kundalini Reiki
Lightarian Reiki
Magnussa Phoenix Reiki
Mari El
Medicine Buddha Reiki
Medicine Dharma Reiki
Medicine Reiki
Monastic Seven Degree Reiki
New Life Reiki
Ni Kawa Reiki
Osho Neo Reiki
Radiance Technique
Rainbow Reiki
Raku Reiki
Reiki Jin Kei Do
Reiki Plus
Rei Ki Tummo
Sacred Path Reiki
Sai baba Reiki
Saku Reiki
Satya Japanese Reiki
Shakyamuni Reiki
Siddhearta Reiki
Silverwolf Reiki
Seichim or Seichem
Sun Li Chung Reiki
Tanaki Reiki
Tera-Mai
Tera-Mai Seichim
Tibetan Soul Star Reiki
Tibetan Reiki
Universal Reiki Dharma
Usui-Do
Usui Reiki Ryoho
Usui Shiki Ryoho
Usui Teate Reiki
Usui/Tibetan Reiki
Usui Universal Healing Reiki
Vajra Reiki
Violet Flame Reiki
Wei Chi Tibetan Reiki

# SEICHIM AND USUI REIKI

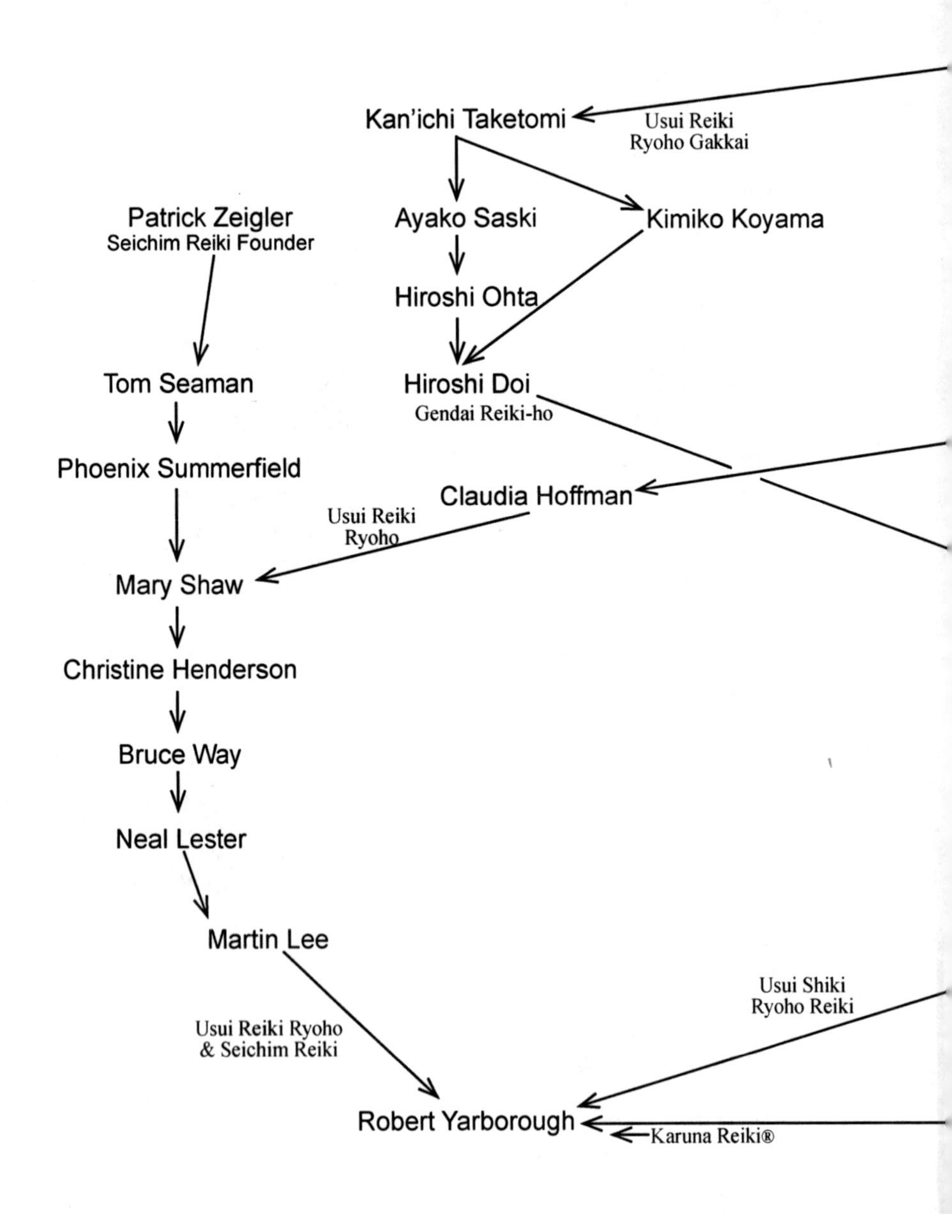

# Usui and Karuna® Reiki

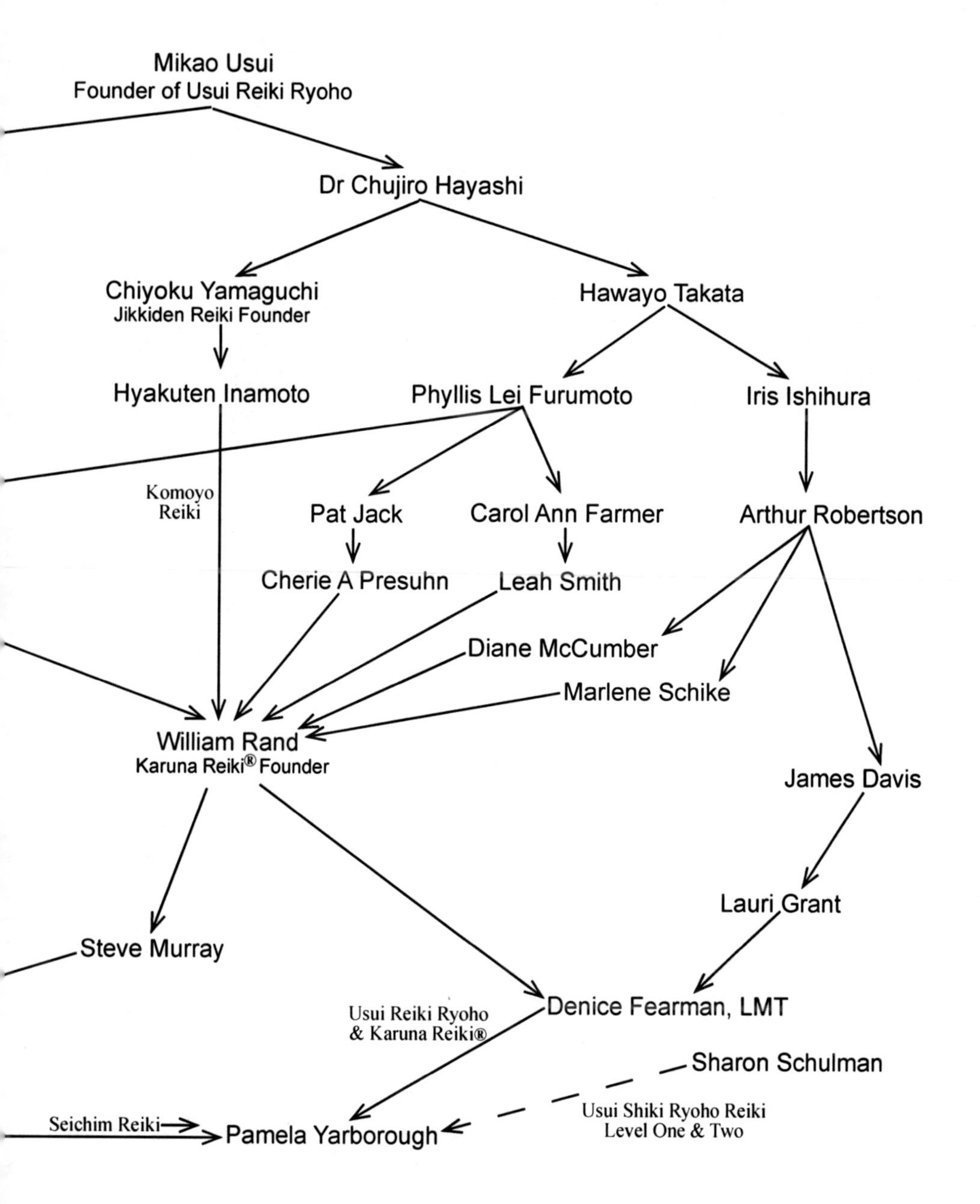

# The Authors

## Robert and Pamela Yarborough

Robert and Pamela are both Master/Teachers in Usui Reiki Ryoho, Seichim Reiki, and Karuna Reiki® and are certified Master Herbalists and Brain Integration Therapists.

As North Carolina State licensed Therapeutic Care Givers, Robert and Pamela worked with children diagnosed with Attention Deficit Hyperactivity Disorder (ADHD) and Attention Deficit Disorder (ADD) for the Cumberland County Mental Health and the Rambaugh Mental Health Center.

Pamela is the former owner of *ACORNS, A Journal of Alternative Homeschooling*, and has written numerous articles on natural healing, homeschooling, and folk traditions for several newsletters and magazines including: *The Mountain Voice, Crow Speaks, The Cottage* and *HICK: Hags in the Country and Kin*, and *The Castroville Times.*

Pamela Yarborough

Actively involved in homeschooling since 1998, Pamela is currenly the chief administrator for Spiral Academy, a private umbrella school for homeschooling families, and was also the co-founder of the Prattville Area Home Educators homeschool cooperative in Alabama.

Pamela's undergraduate work was in psychology and in the metaphysical arts, and she holds a Doctorate of Naturopathy. She is also a certified Scuba Diver and Taekwondo Master Instructor with a 4th Dan (degree) black belt from the World Taekwondo Federation (Kukkiwon) and a 1st Dan in Combat Hapkido.

Robert is a retired Air Force Lieutenant Colonel, instructor pilot, and combat veteran of Bosnia-Herzegovina and the Gulf War. He has logged over 5000 flight hours in 16 different types of military and civilian aircraft including helicopters, supersonic jets, transports, aerobatic trainers, light twins, and gliders.

Robert's last assignment was as the commander of the Rocky Mountain Liaison Region covering Colorado, Wyoming, Utah, Idaho, and Montana as the Air Force's senior advisor to the AF Auxiliary (Civil Air Patrol) in the region. During his 25 years of service, he lived abroad for 8 years and traveled to over 45 countries including Japan, Korean, Germany, Morocco, Oman, Jamaica, Bolivia, Spain, Italy, and many others.

Robert studied martial arts for 30 years and actively taught for over 20 of those. Robert holds master level certification in Taekwondo, Tangsoodo, and Combat Hapkido, as well as black belt certification in traditional Hapkido, Jujutsu, and Karate. In 1997 he was an International Martial Arts Hall of Fame inductee as Instructor of the Year.

Robert Yarborough

In addition to his work in the Martial Arts and the Air Force, Robert is a certified Scuba diver and award winning photographer with hundreds of images published in international newspapers, magazines and books, including 8 cover photos.

Robert holds a Bachelors of Professional Aeronautics and a masters in Computer Resources and Information Management.

Pamela and Robert have been married for over 20 years and currently reside in Colorado with the three youngest of their five children.

# INDEX

## S

# *Order Additional Copies Today!*

Reiki is an ancient system of healing through the "laying on of hands" that is simple enough for children of all ages to learn. The Children's Reiki Handbook is a guide to energy healing that provides kids with the information they need to prepare for their First-, Second- and Master Level Reiki Attunements; and shows them how to use their new skills to heal themselves and others.

This guide also includes: Healing with Reiki, Attunements; how to prepare for them and what to expect, Chakras and Auras...and more.

ISBN : 978-0-9774181-5-2
paperback

*Only*
*$17.^{95}$*

*"I found Children's Reiki Handbook to be a concise yet thorough introduction to the Usui healing system of Reiki. It's perfect for children and young adults"*

- ML Rhodes, Reiki Master/Teacher (Usui Ryoho, Sehkim, and Karuna Reiki), and Amazon #1 Best Selling Author

*"If you want to learn Reiki, this book will serve as in inspiration towards that goal... This Reiki handbook is a great resource to introduce the benefits of Reiki healing to children or grown ups who are just starting out."*

- Erin Kelly-Allshouse, *Children of the New Earth*

**You can download an order form at our website or call toll free to order any of our books. We accept all major credit cards:**

**www.Andborough.com**

CPSIA information can be obtained at www.ICGtesting.com
Printed in the USA
BVOW03s1031011014

369056BV00004B/114/P